The Future of
U.S. Special Operations Forces

**COUNCIL *on*
FOREIGN
RELATIONS**

Council Special Report No. 66
April 2013

Linda Robinson

The Future of
U.S. Special Operations Forces

The Council on Foreign Relations (CFR) is an independent, nonpartisan membership organization, think tank, and publisher dedicated to being a resource for its members, government officials, business executives, journalists, educators and students, civic and religious leaders, and other interested citizens in order to help them better understand the world and the foreign policy choices facing the United States and other countries. Founded in 1921, CFR carries out its mission by maintaining a diverse membership, with special programs to promote interest and develop expertise in the next generation of foreign policy leaders; convening meetings at its headquarters in New York and in Washington, DC, and other cities where senior government officials, members of Congress, global leaders, and prominent thinkers come together with Council members to discuss and debate major international issues; supporting a Studies Program that fosters independent research, enabling CFR scholars to produce articles, reports, and books and hold roundtables that analyze foreign policy issues and make concrete policy recommendations; publishing *Foreign Affairs*, the preeminent journal on international affairs and U.S. foreign policy; sponsoring Independent Task Forces that produce reports with both findings and policy prescriptions on the most important foreign policy topics; and providing up-to-date information and analysis about world events and American foreign policy on its website, CFR.org.

The Council on Foreign Relations takes no institutional positions on policy issues and has no affiliation with the U.S. government. All views expressed in its publications and on its website are the sole responsibility of the author or authors.

Council Special Reports (CSRs) are concise policy briefs, produced to provide a rapid response to a developing crisis or contribute to the public's understanding of current policy dilemmas. CSRs are written by individual authors—who may be CFR fellows or acknowledged experts from outside the institution—in consultation with an advisory committee, and are intended to take sixty days from inception to publication. The committee serves as a sounding board and provides feedback on a draft report. It usually meets twice— once before a draft is written and once again when there is a draft for review; however, advisory committee members, unlike Task Force members, are not asked to sign off on the report or to otherwise endorse it. Once published, CSRs are posted on www.cfr.org.

For further information about CFR or this Special Report, please write to the Council on Foreign Relations, 58 East 68th Street, New York, NY 10065, or call the Communications office at 212.434.9888. Visit our website, CFR.org.

Copyright © 2013 by the Council on Foreign Relations®, Inc.
All rights reserved.
Printed in the United States of America.

This report may not be reproduced in whole or in part, in any form beyond the reproduction permitted by Sections 107 and 108 of the U.S. Copyright Law Act (17 U.S.C. Sections 107 and 108) and excerpts by reviewers for the public press, without express written permission from the Council on Foreign Relations.

To submit a letter in response to a Council Special Report for publication on our website, CFR.org, you may send an email to CSReditor@cfr.org. Alternatively, letters may be mailed to us at: Publications Department, Council on Foreign Relations, 58 East 68th Street, New York, NY 10065. Letters should include the writer's name, postal address, and daytime phone number. Letters may be edited for length and clarity, and may be published online. Please do not send attachments. All letters become the property of the Council on Foreign Relations and will not be returned. We regret that, owing to the volume of correspondence, we cannot respond to every letter.

Contents

Foreword vii
Acknowledgments ix

Council Special Report 1
Introduction 3
Special Operations Forces and the Strategic Context 5
Special Operations Forces Organization and Missions 8
Shortfalls in Special Operations Forces 13
Recommendations 20
Conclusion 26

Appendix 28
Endnotes 30
About the Author 33
Advisory Committee 34

Foreword

U.S. special operations forces are doing more things in more places than ever before. They are now active in some seventy countries and, since 2001, have seen their combined budget nearly quintuple—a trend that seems likely to continue. As the United States seeks ways to tackle a range of security threats worldwide, shore up the resilience of its friends and allies against terrorist and criminal networks, and minimize need for large-scale military interventions, the importance of special operations forces will grow.

Yet, writes Linda Robinson in this Council Special Report, the strategic vision for special operations forces has not kept pace with the growing demands for their skills. Most people—and, indeed, many policymakers—associate the special operations forces with secret nighttime raids like the one that targeted Osama bin Laden: tactical operations against a particular individual or group. The abilities of special operations forces, however, extend much further, into military training, information operations, civilian affairs, and more. As the United States shifts its focus from war fighting to building and supporting its partners, Robinson argues, it will become critical to better define these strategic capabilities and ensure that special operations forces have the staffing and funding to succeed. Robinson further calls on the Pentagon to remove bureaucratic and operational obstacles to cooperation among the special operations forces of each service, and between special and conventional forces. She also recommends that all special operations forces commands work to develop a pipeline of talented, motivated officers with expertise in these issues, and that the role of civilian leadership in budget and operational oversight be reinforced.

The Future of U.S. Special Operations Forces is a timely report on the future of what may become the military's most important troops. It offers a broad set of recommendations covering institutional, operational, and intellectual reforms that could improve the versatility and effectiveness of the special operations forces. As the Pentagon seeks new ways to exert American power in an era of lower budgets and higher aversion to wars on the scale of Iraq and Afghanistan, this report argues that expanding the role of special operations forces can—and should—be high on the agenda.

Richard N. Haass
President
Council on Foreign Relations
April 2013

Acknowledgments

I would like to thank CFR President Richard N. Haass and Director of Studies James M. Lindsay for supporting this study and providing an intellectually stimulating and hospitable environment in which to conduct it. I am grateful to the many senior and rising special operations leaders and numerous policy officials who gave generously of their time in interviews for this project. Over sixty interviews were conducted as part of the project's data-gathering phase. Although this endeavor was conducted as an independent study, U.S. Special Operations Command provided data and permitted officers to be interviewed. The interview subjects were all granted anonymity to ensure the greatest candor possible. A number of these individuals also participated in a CFR roundtable series to discuss the major topics identified in the research phase, along with congressional staff, academic experts, and members of the wider interagency policy community. These sessions were designed to foster an in-depth dialogue about the role of special operations forces in national security strategy. The rich discussions and conversations with House and Senate Armed Services Committee staff members and other experts also informed my thinking and the contours of the report.

Special thanks are due to the members of the excellent advisory committee that was convened to review this Council Special Report, in particular retired ambassador James F. Dobbins, who served as its chair. The committee members reviewed an outline and a draft of the report in two sessions and offered insightful comments that greatly improved the final product.

Research Associate Jane McMurrey was my indispensable partner throughout this project; I cannot thank her enough for her multiple contributions in research and organizational support. She kept the project on track during my extensive international travel to observe special operations forces in the field. The highly professional members of CFR's Washington and New York offices and the Studies Program staff were a pleasure to work with. I would like to thank in particular Patricia Dorff and her Publications team, Jean-Michel Oriol and the Finance team, and Lisa Shields and the Global Communications and Media Relations team. This project was made possible by a grant from the Smith Richardson Foundation. The statements made and views expressed herein are solely my own.

Linda Robinson

Council Special Report

Introduction

The United States has arrived at a critical inflection point in the development and employment of its special operations forces. Budget pressures and exhaustion with large-scale wars now place a new premium on small-footprint operations and partnering with allies to provide cost-effective defense. Special operations forces are uniquely designed to play both of those roles. Therefore, given the likely ongoing heavy reliance on special operations forces, it is imperative that national security policymakers and defense officials ensure that these forces are prepared to perform their full range of missions. The strategic context is now shifting, and adjustments are in order. Al-Qaeda has been degraded severely, although offshoots remain potent threats. Unless another major war erupts, U.S. special operations forces are unlikely to continue the intensive pace of raids—often a dozen or more a night—as they have done in recent years in Afghanistan and Iraq.

Over the past decade, special operations forces have honed their counterterrorism manhunting ability and notched significant operational successes, most prominently in the mission that killed al-Qaeda founder and leader Osama bin Laden. These unilateral manhunting skills represent only one of their two basic capabilities—albeit the one that has understandably received the most attention and resources in recent years. Their other capability is developing and working alongside indigenous forces to combat terrorists, insurgents, and transnational criminal networks through an orchestrated set of defense, information, and civil affairs programs. Special operations leaders often say that the unilateral or "direct" approach buys time for the longer-term "indirect" approach to work, and that the latter is decisive in addressing a threat. This indirect approach has been successfully applied over the past decade in Colombia and the Philippines, where small numbers of army, navy, air force, and marine special operators have worked with indigenous counterparts to greatly diminish the threats in both countries, as part of a multifaceted country assistance program. To be successful, this application of special operations requires both sustained commitment and coordinated effort, yet that is rarely achieved. The "indirect approach" has not been prioritized, and the orchestration of special operations capabilities in sustained efforts remains the most serious operational deficit.

Given that special operations forces have become the tool of choice to deal with many national security threats, it is vital that this deficit be remedied to ensure that their unique and varied capabilities are employed to their fullest and most enduring effect. An enormous investment has been made in expanding and equipping special operations forces over the past decade. They have doubled in size and been deployed more often and for longer periods than ever before. They have more generals and admirals leading their ranks—almost seventy, compared with nine a dozen years ago. However, since these advances have been made, there has been no thoroughgoing official assessment of the results of this growth and increased employment, due in part to the press of wartime demands. Special operators often say that they are a tactical-sized force that can have strategic impact, yet precisely how they are to achieve that impact and whether they do so remain undefined. Despite the enormous growth and increased pace of activity, far too often special operations forces have been employed in tactical and episodic ways, and many opportunities for achieving greater cooperation among their component parts or with others have been missed.

Adopting a new vision for special operations forces that shifts from a tactical focus on removing individuals from a battlefield to a focus on achieving sustained political-military effect will require a shift in priorities and a concomitant rebalancing of the budget. Without these improvements, special operations forces will remain largely a tactical force that achieves limited rather than enduring or decisive effects in confronting terrorism, insurgencies, and other irregular threats.

Special Operations Forces and the Strategic Context

Special operations forces comprise a wide variety of carefully selected and highly trained units from all four U.S. military services, with different histories and different competencies. Army special operations forces comprise half of all special operators and include the largest and oldest element of U.S. special operations forces, the Special Forces, which are recognizable by their green berets, as well as Rangers, aviators, civil affairs soldiers, and psychological operations troops. The navy special operations forces include the well-known SEALs (Sea, Air, Land), which marked their fiftieth anniversary in 2012, and the marines special operations command, which was formed in 2006. The air force special operations command includes both pilots and ground personnel.

Two principal features of the domestic and international environment forecast the likelihood of ongoing high demand for special operations forces to achieve U.S. national security objectives: U.S. budgetary pressures and the continued prevalence of irregular threats. The United States will likely face continued fiscal constraints, which place a premium on cost-effective approaches to national security. In January 2012, the Obama administration issued new defense strategic guidance that, among other things, prioritized ongoing counterterrorism efforts and the adoption of "innovative, low-cost, and small-footprint approaches to achieve security objectives."[1]

One of the most cost-effective elements of the defense arsenal, special operators are mature and highly skilled. They are selected and trained to deploy in very small numbers, whether conducting unilateral missions or working with foreign partners. The special operations budget for the 2012 fiscal year was $10.5 billion, 1.4 percent of the total defense budget. Including the amount that the military services contribute to special operations for such things as personnel and standard-issue equipment, the total comes to 4 percent of defense spending—a fairly small percentage in relation to the contribution of special operations forces to national security objectives. Though the special operations budget has more than quadrupled from $2.3 billion in 2001, the growth leveled off with a budget request of $10.4 billion for the 2013 fiscal year.[2]

The other reason to expect a high demand for special operations forces is the continuing prevalence of irregular threats to U.S. national security, the types of threats that these forces are designed to address. The defense strategic guidance and other intelligence assessments forecast ongoing irregular threats by nonstate actors such as terrorists, insurgents, and transnational criminal networks that are increasingly empowered by technology and other forces of globalization. Though the core al-Qaeda organization has been degraded, its affiliates have grown and spread to other unstable, ungoverned, or conflict-ridden areas in the Middle East and Africa. State adversaries are also likely to resort to unconventional tactics to counter the overwhelmingly superior conventional power of the United States and its allies.[3]

Though the future portends ongoing high demand for special operations forces, it is important to note that they are a scarce resource. They constitute less than 5 percent of total U.S. military forces, so they cannot be employed everywhere. Many U.S. partner-building and military activities can and should be carried out by conventional forces. Special operations forces are designed for missions that conventional forces cannot undertake, such as those that require operating in a low-profile manner, behind enemy lines, or in politically sensitive places.[4] They are also ideally suited to work with other countries' special operations forces.

Small-footprint special operations missions will likely run a wide gamut in the future. Due to the end of the U.S. combat role in Afghanistan and the weakening of the core al-Qaeda organization, unilateral counterterrorism missions may evolve from high-tempo missions in a few countries to far fewer but more geographically diffuse operations conducted against those who represent dire and imminent threats to U.S. interests. Authorities and procedures for this unilateral application of force beyond declared theaters of war will have to be clarified. In the absence of another major war, it is likely that special operations will increasingly focus on enabling or empowering other countries' forces to address threats within their own borders. In many cases, this effort may be a multinational one that includes an expanding network of special operations partners around the globe, a number of which U.S. special operators have formed, trained, and/or mentored. For example, beyond traditional partners such as Britain, Australia, and Canada, the network now includes Colombia, Jordan, the United Arab Emirates, and countries in eastern Europe.

Special Operations Forces Organization and Missions

Special operations forces have a complex organization, a diverse set of capabilities, and a broad range of officially assigned missions, all of which can make it difficult to understand exactly who special operations forces are and how they should be used. In many respects, it is a relatively new community, one that is still in the process of formulating in-depth answers to the questions of "who they are" and "what they do." An outline of the organizational structure and missions provides a baseline for the discussion of a new operating model; shortfalls in the current conceptual, operational, and institutional development; and potential remedies.

WHO SPECIAL OPERATIONS FORCES ARE

In 1987, all of the military services' separate special operations units were brought together under the newly formed U.S. Special Operations Command (USSOCOM), which was created by congressional fiat over military objections after an extensive inquiry into the failed operation to rescue American hostages in Iran. Congress also created a new Pentagon office, that of the assistant secretary of defense for special operations/low-intensity conflict, which is charged with overseeing policy and resources for special operations/low-intensity conflict and advising the secretary of defense on special operations.[5]

Table 1 outlines the special operations forces command structure and assigned personnel. The four-star U.S. Special Operations Command consists of four service components and one subordinate unified command, Joint Special Operations Command. The U.S. military splits regional oversight of U.S. military activity around the world into six geographic combatant commands that are each overseen by a four-star

TABLE 1: USSOCOM PERSONNEL MANNING BY ORGANIZATION

Organization	Number of Personnel	Percentage of USSOCOM
U.S. Special Operations Command Headquarters	2,606	4.0
U.S. Army Special Operations Command	28,500	45.0
Air Force Special Operations Command	18,000	28.0
Naval Special Warfare Command	9,000	14.0
U.S. Marine Corps Forces Special Operations Command	2,600	4.0
Joint Special Operations Command HQ	1,519	2.4
Theater Special Operations Command HQs	1,425	2.2
Total	63,650	100.0

Source: USSOCOM. Numbers approximate as of August 2012.

general or admiral. Within those geographic combatant commands, theater special operations commands (TSOCs) functioned as subordinate unified commands to oversee special operations activities.[6] A recent change converted these six theater special operations commands into subordinate unified commands of U.S. Special Operations Command. In this new configuration, U.S. Special Operations Command will assume a greater role in preparing and supporting the theater special operations commands, but the geographic combatant commands will continue to exercise operational control over them, planning and directing their operations. (It is important for the geographic combatant commands to retain operational control, since TSOC operations should always be conceived and executed as part of the plan of the geographic combatant command to ensure synergy and effectiveness.)

The total number of personnel assigned to U.S. Special Operations Command and its constituent units for the 2013 fiscal year is 66,594, including both civilian and uniformed personnel. Of that number, approximately thirty-three thousand are special operators. Currently, twelve thousand of those operators are deployed at any one time; about half are in Afghanistan and the remainder are dispersed in seventy-odd countries. U.S. Special Operations Command plans to reach a total of seventy-one thousand personnel during the 2015 fiscal year, but budgetary considerations may affect further expansion. (The appendix lists the special operations units and their approximate assigned manpower.)

WHAT SPECIAL OPERATIONS FORCES DO

Americans are likely familiar with two iconic special operations missions of the past decade: the toppling of the Taliban regime by bearded army Special Forces and air force special operators who joined ranks with Afghan militias after the 9/11 attacks, and the daring raid in Pakistan by navy SEALs that killed Osama bin Laden in May 2011. Apart from these high-profile missions, most Americans are not aware of how widely and intensively special operations forces have been employed, or of how diverse their missions are. Although they do indeed conduct raids against terrorists and insurgents, they also carry out a range of advisory, information, intelligence, and civil affairs missions.

Special operations forces are assigned to conduct a variety of missions under U.S. law (Title 10, Section 167) and military doctrine (Joint Publication 3-05). Special operations forces are to be prepared to undertake the following eleven "core operations and activities": counterinsurgency, counterterrorism, counterproliferation of weapons of mass destruction, foreign internal defense, security force assistance, unconventional warfare, direct action, special reconnaissance, information operations, military information support operations, and civil affairs operations.[7] This official list of missions includes disparate and overlapping elements and does not therefore constitute an easily accessible guide to what special operations forces do.[8]

In recent years, the special operations leadership has developed a formulation to convey that special operations forces are employed in essentially two modes—a direct approach of unilateral manhunting (such as the raid that brought down bin Laden) and an indirect approach of working through and with others (such as the decade-long effort to build competent special operations forces and counternarcotics police in Colombia and assist the country's counterinsurgency effort). In the command's official annual posture statement to Congress in March 2012, USSOCOM commander Admiral William H. McRaven provided this description of the direct and indirect approaches:

> The direct approach is characterized by technologically enabled small-unit precision lethality, focused intelligence, and interagency cooperation integrated on a digitally networked battlefield. . . . The direct approach alone is not the solution to the

challenges our nation faces today, as it ultimately only buys time and space for the indirect approach and broader governmental elements to take effect. Less well-known but decisive in importance, the indirect approach is the complementary element that can counter the systemic components of the threat.

The indirect approach includes empowering host nation forces, providing appropriate assistance to humanitarian agencies, and engaging key populations. These long-term efforts increase partner capabilities to generate sufficient security and rule of law, address local needs, and advance ideas that discredit and defeat the appeal of violent extremism.... One way [special operations forces achieves] this goal through the indirect approach is through forward and persistent engagement of key countries. Small in scale by design, this engagement directly supports the country teams' and [geographic combatant commands'] theater plans to counter threats to stability.[9]

This formulation of the direct and indirect approaches represented an effort to clarify what U.S. special operations do. Although the special operations community now uses the terms *direct approach* and *indirect approach*, it does not always use them consistently. Moreover, conventional forces and others in government do not always understand them, because they are not part of the wider military lexicon or doctrine. The main problem with the terms *direct* and *indirect* is that they are vague. Recognizing this, in 2012 the army adopted *surgical strike* and *special warfare* as more descriptive terms.[10]

Whether they are called the direct approach or surgical strikes, unilateral raids are a fairly simple concept to grasp. The meaning of the term *indirect approach* (or *special warfare*) is less clear, since it encompasses a multiplicity of activities. The unifying element of these activities is political-military warfare, or shaping and influencing environments and populations. In carrying out this indirect approach, special operations forces may train and advise armies, police forces, informal militias, tribes, and civil defense forces. They can do this advisory work in a variety of ways. For example, they may be combat advisers carrying guns in the field alongside a partner force; be restricted to supplying direct assistance, such as airlift or intelligence in the field; or only conduct training in special operations techniques.

Though special operators most often work with military or police units, on occasion they work directly with civilians. In Afghanistan, as in Vietnam, special operators are working with tribal elders, local governments, and civilian volunteers to form village defense forces. Along with multinational special operations partners, special operators are also training special police units and conducting operations alongside Afghan commandos and Special Forces.

Finally, special operations forces may engage in nonlethal activities such as dispute resolution at the village level, the collecting or disseminating of information, or civil affairs projects such as medical or veterinary aid and building schools or wells. Persuasion and influence are part of many of these operations, and the long-term effect is to build relationships and partnerships that endure. In many cases, these partners become part of alliance or coalition efforts elsewhere in the world. Whether the partner forces merely secure their own countries or become part of wider security partnerships, these relationships are the most powerful enduring effect that special operations can aim to achieve.

Shortfalls in Special Operations Forces

For special operations forces to progress from a largely tactical tool to one that regularly achieves or contributes substantially to decisive and enduring effects, they must adopt a new model with two essential features. The first is a shift to make developing and operating with partners—political-military activity in all its diverse forms—their central means of achieving lasting effect. The second is adoption of a systematic approach that routinely combines their diverse special operations capabilities—civil affairs, informational, advisory, and so forth—as needed in deliberate campaigns executed over time, in concert with other military and civilian entities. Several shortfalls in special operations theory, organization, and institutional development currently inhibit the forces' ability to plan and operate in this manner.

In its official posture statements and other documents, U.S. Special Operations Command has attempted to frame a theory of special operations using the terms *direct* and *indirect*, whereby the direct approach "buys time" for the indirect approach to work in a decisive fashion.[11] In other words, raids and strikes are a means to disrupt a threat, while political-military activities are undertaken by special operations forces (and others) to address the threat in a more lasting manner. Though this formulation holds that the indirect approach is the decisive element, it has not been prioritized in practice. The lion's share of attention, effort, and resources in the past decade has been devoted to honing and applying the direct approach. In fact, both the general public and many policymakers now equate special operations forces almost exclusively with the direct approach. The net result is that special operations forces are stuck conducting endless strikes on terrorist target lists that are consistently repopulated with new individuals, with no theory or measure to determine whether or when a network is sufficiently degraded to no longer constitute a threat. And the indirect approach languishes more as a bumper sticker or a random engagement tool than an overarching game-changing approach that effectively addresses conflicts or emerging threats.

This is not a formula for the optimum employment of special operations forces. The root issue is conceptual clarity about how these forces should be used to best effect (i.e., a scarce asset to be employed to accomplish ends that no other military force can achieve). Without greater clarity, there is a serious danger that special operations forces will be employed in a permanent global game of whack-a-mole and in other tactical and episodic ways, rather than as part of deliberate campaigns that can achieve lasting outcomes. In addition, the special operations community is not organized to implement such orchestrated and linked special operations activities, and it has not oriented its institutions to make this its central priority.

CONCEPTUAL SHORTFALLS

The principal conceptual shortfall is the lack of a clear and coherent lexicon and doctrine that explain what special operations forces do and how they are to be employed. The ways in which they achieve their effects have not been fleshed out into a template that can be adapted and applied to various cases and explained in a way that is readily understood and embraced by policymakers and other partners in government. Special operations forces should also be a fount of innovative ideas for addressing unconventional and emerging threats. Developing special operations forces' intellectual capital has not been prioritized, as the focus to date has been on finding and fixing individual targets. Thus, it is of small wonder that, without this foundation, special operations forces have been characteristically employed in tactical and episodic ways. Over the course of a given year, they are deployed to as many as one hundred countries, mostly for short periods, but only in a few of those cases do their activities have a decisive or enduring impact. A new model for employing special operations forces would follow the approach used in Colombia and the Philippines, where special operations forces planned ongoing campaigns that use numerous advisory, civil affairs, and informational activities to assess and address those governments' weaknesses in providing security and remedying underlying sources of conflict. The operators developed these plans in coordination with the Colombian and Philippine governments and integrated them into the geographic combatant command theater plans, as well as the U.S. embassies' country plans. Finally, operators coordinated their activities with other relevant joint forces and civilian efforts.

OPERATIONAL SHORTFALLS

The most glaring and critical operational deficit is the fact that, according to doctrine, the theater special operations commands are supposed to be the principal node for planning and conducting special operations in a given theater—yet they are the most severely underresourced commands. Rather than world-class integrators of direct and indirect capabilities, theater special operations commands are egregiously short of sufficient quantity and quality of staff and intelligence, analytical, and planning resources. They are also supposed to be the principal advisers on special operations to their respective geographic combatant commanders, but they rarely have received the respect and support of the four-star command. The latter often redirects resources and staff that are supposed to go to the theater special operations commands, which routinely receive about 20 percent fewer personnel than they have been formally assigned.[12] Furthermore, career promotions from TSOC staff jobs are rare, which makes those assignments unattractive and results in a generally lower-quality workforce. Finally, a high proportion of the personnel are on short-term assignment or are reservists with inadequate training. Because of this lack of resources, theater special operations commands have been unable to fulfill their role of planning and conducting special operations.

The second operational shortfall is the lack of unity of command. Special operations forces have been routinely employed for the past decade under separate organizations that operate under separate chains of command, even within the same country. Unity of command, which holds that all forces should operate under a single command structure to best employ them in pursuit of a common objective, is a basic principle of military operations. Only once, in Afghanistan beginning in July 2012, have all special operations units in one country been brought together under one command. This should become standard procedure in new theaters such as Yemen and Africa, as the ideal means to cooperate internally and with other partners. Except for large-scale special operations efforts such as in Afghanistan, the logical entities to exercise command over all special operations units are the theater special operations commands. This should be standard for any units operating in a persistent manner. Even discrete, time-limited operations by special mission units should be coordinated and their potential effects on the wider effort assessed. The existence of two separate special operations organizations with headquarters in the field creates internal frictions and makes coordination with conventional commanders, U.S. embassies, and host-nation governments even more complex and fraught with potential misunderstandings.

The third operational shortfall is the lack of a mechanism to ensure that sustained special operations activities in a given country are funded consistently. It makes little difference if a coherent special operations plan is devised if its component activities to achieve lasting effect over time lack consistent funding. Most special operations—even those conducted in a single country—are funded in piecemeal fashion to support a given activity with a given partner force for a certain mission or time period.[13] Additionally, proposals for a given training or advisory activity must compete in a lottery for funding each year, creating a degree of uncertainty that can disrupt operations and partnerships. Some of these authorities require the approval of the Department of State, which can take up to two years to secure. Developing and operating with partners is a long-term endeavor that requires a sustained commitment if it is to produce the desired results, such as those achieved in Colombia and the Philippines.

In addition to these internal operational shortfalls, special operations forces and conventional military forces have failed to combine routinely in ways that would increase the U.S. capacity to conduct small-footprint operations. Special operations forces lack enablers (such as airlift, combat aviation, logistics, intelligence, surveillance, and reconnaissance, and special functions such as judge advocates and provost marshals), additional infantry, and command relationships. By design and doctrine, special operations forces rely on the conventional military. Conventional forces do not readily provide small, scalable units because their systems are geared toward providing larger units. This is a consequence of preparing to fight large, conventional wars and is a primary impediment to the agility needed in this era of dynamic, hybrid threats. The problem extends beyond the enabler shortfall. If a more flexible system could be developed, the two forces could combine in creative new ways. For example, in an experiment under way in

Afghanistan, two conventional infantry battalions have been attached to special operations forces and split into squads to help carry out the village stability operations. Such blended combinations of special operations and conventional forces would extend the U.S. military's capacity to conduct small-footprint missions in various places. But the necessary training, command, and habitual relationships among the two forces are lacking—and beneath that is a continuing reluctance to make the changes necessary to institutionalize and improve such innovations.

INSTITUTIONAL SHORTFALLS

The final set of deficiencies to inhibit the further development of special operations forces is institutional. The parent U.S. Special Operations Command has not adequately fulfilled its two primary institutional responsibilities: to prepare special operations personnel at senior levels and provide special operations strategy and doctrine. On the first count, it has not provided adequate career management and education to prepare its leaders to guide the future of special operations forces and compete for relevant senior joint positions. One major impediment is that the military services control career assignments and promotions; U.S. Special Operations Command has only monitoring responsibilities under U.S. law (Title 10, Section 167). On the second count, it has failed to develop and disseminate a clear and pathbreaking doctrine for strategic employment of special operations forces. One little-known reason for this is the low density of special operations forces expertise at USSOCOM headquarters; special operations personnel constitute only 11 percent of the workforce.

More broadly, however, these institutional tasks of personnel and doctrine development have not been sufficiently valued in what might be termed the "operator culture" of the special operations community. One manifestation of this has been U.S. Special Operations Command's recurring bid to increase its operational role rather than attend to these vital institutional needs of leadership and doctrine development that will ultimately do more to create world-class special operations capabilities. According to U.S. law (Title 10, Section 167), U.S. Special Operations Command may play an operational role if requested by the secretary of defense or the president. In the wake of the 9/11 attacks, the secretary of defense designated U.S. Special Operations Command as the lead command for the war on terror, but the geographic combatant commanders resisted what they viewed as an incursion into their geographic purview. USSOCOM headquarters staff nearly doubled, and an expensive operations center was built in anticipation of a role that was never assumed. U.S. Special Operations Command continues to advocate for a role in addressing global threats that cross these geographic boundaries and avers that geographic combatant commanders do not understand or employ special operations forces effectively. It is critical to delineate a workable division of labor and develop mechanisms for ensuring that the four-star commands cooperate with rather than stymie each other. One core function of U.S. Special Operations Command should be to ensure that geographic combatant command staffs, which rotate every few years, understand special operations forces and how to employ them.

In the Pentagon, the Office of the Assistant Secretary of Defense for Special Operations/Low-Intensity Conflict has difficulty fully providing civilian oversight of U.S. Special Operations Command's policy and resources, as directed by law.[14] Relative to the importance of special operations in current U.S. defense strategy, the office is understaffed and lacks Department of Defense–relevant policy expertise. Furthermore, the assistant secretary is often seen only as an advocate for and arm of U.S. Special Operations Command rather than as an independent source of advice and expertise, which undercuts its effectiveness as the secretary's principal civilian adviser on special operations. One of two main shortfalls has been in exercising its statutory oversight of resources: its role in determining resourcing levels and priorities—which is central to executing policy and driving change in any organization—has been eclipsed by U.S. Special Operations Command's creation of a three-star vice commander in Washington whose portfolio is resources. The second major shortfall has been in providing adequate policy oversight, advice, and coordination across the full range of special operations' assigned missions. In the past decade, the office has focused overwhelmingly on counterterrorism and operational and even tactical matters rather than on policy and strategy for the entire special operations/low-intensity conflict spectrum. In addition, the office's portfolio has evolved to include areas other than special operations/low-intensity conflict, which has drained scarce staff attention. Counternarcotics and a variety of other responsibilities have been given to this office, which has been reorganized in every presidential administration. The combined effect has been to undermine effective oversight of both resources and policy.

The law assigns a supervisory function to the Office of the Assistant Secretary of Defense for Special Operations/Low-Intensity Conflict, as well as a role in establishing policy for special operations. Thus, policy deliberations on whether and when to employ special operations forces ought to be the dominant focus of the assistant secretary, along with the subsequent planning, coordination, and implementation of any resulting policy decisions with all relevant U.S. government agencies. Given the broad and varied application of special operations and how little they are understood, it is imperative that the secretary of defense has a well-staffed source of expertise on which to rely. In addition, the recurrent concerns expressed by legislators, the media, and others about special operations forces operating outside the bounds of civilian control and oversight should be addressed in the first instance with robust and effective policy oversight by the Office of the Assistant Secretary of Defense for Special Operations/Low-Intensity Conflict.

If a new model of applying special operations forces as part of sustained campaigns is adopted, along the lines of Colombia, it would imply an increased demand for policy input and oversight. For example, special operations may now be required across a large portion of North Africa as weak governments struggle to find their footing and militant groups proliferate. In all such cases, the assistant secretary of defense for special operations/low-intensity conflict should play a major role in shaping an effective policy, along with the State Department and the regional assistant secretaries at the Pentagon. In part due to the short and inadequate staffing at the Office of the Assistant Secretary of Defense for Special Operations/Low-Intensity Conflict, U.S. Special Operations Command has moved to fill the vacuum by creating new coordination structures in Washington. Policy planning should be followed by operational planning and coordination; the latter should not supplant the former.

Recommendations

The following conceptual, operational, and institutional changes, to be accomplished through a rebalancing of resources, will enable special operations forces to retool and provide even more effective security solutions at lower cost. These changes will raise the level of special operations forces' ability to develop and work with a variety of partner forces and enable them to routinely combine their own diverse capabilities to achieve maximum impact, and in this way progress beyond their current tactical plateau.

DEVELOP INTELLECTUAL CAPITAL AND LEADERS

The two most important steps that the special operations community can take to ensure that special operations mature are develop intellectual capital and produce strategic-minded leaders. These two issues are linked, since senior leaders are responsible for setting the community's direction and ensuring that it becomes an adaptive learning organization. Leaders need a deep understanding of the full range of special operations capabilities and a broad understanding of national security policymaking to guide their community. That same background will also qualify senior special operations leaders for relevant senior joint assignments. To achieve these goals, U.S. Special Operations Command should

- produce a doctrine for special operations that describes how special operations forces achieve decisive or enduring impact through the surgical application of force coupled with long-term campaigns of enabling and operating with a variety of partners, in conjunction with other government agencies. This doctrine should include a theory of special operations that describes how they can achieve strategic or decisive impact, particularly by affecting the political level of war. In some cases, a raid or series of raids may be decisive in dealing a knockout blow to a terrorist network, for example, but more often an extended effort on multiple fronts will be required to address the threat's ability to regenerate. The body of thought should also include sound methods for assessing complex conflict dynamics and conducting campaigns of influence and persuasion that factor in the differing interests of the other parties and determine the likelihood of and means by which a positive outcome may be achieved. Finally, it should describe how such efforts can be conducted as combined endeavors.[15]

- ensure that promotable special operations personnel are assigned to relevant joint and interagency positions beyond the counterterrorism positions currently filled—including the National Security Council staff, the State Department's Bureau of Conflict and Stabilization Operations, and State and Defense regional bureaus—to increase their understanding of interagency processes and enhance collaboration with the government entities that establish and implement policy.
- request the USSOCOM commander's routine participation in joint assignments and nominations for senior positions in the geographic combatant commands.
- ask Congress to revise U.S. law to grant U.S. Special Operations Command authority to comanage special operations personnel assignments with the services.

IMPROVE CAPACITY FOR LONG-DURATION EFFORTS WITH PARTNERS BY, INTER ALIA, SHIFTING RESOURCES AND PERSONNEL FROM U.S. SPECIAL OPERATIONS COMMAND

To perform their assigned role as the central node for conducting special operations—and as such the main entity that will implement the new combined and partnered operations—theater special operations commands should be provided with sufficient quality staff, resources, and authority to plan and conduct special operations that are fully nested within the geographic combatant commands' theater plans, State Department plans, and national policy. The following recommendations would help achieve this critical organizational and operational objective:

- U.S. Special Operations Command should fully resource theater special operations commands out of its own budget if the needed funding is not provided by the services; transfer billets from U.S. Special Operations Command; increase the quality and quantity of special operations planners, staff, and other experts required to produce detailed and well-grounded contributions to theater campaign plans; revise promotion precepts to incentivize TSOC service; and prioritize collaboration with the wider geographic combatant command staff. Currently, U.S. Special Operations Command plans to increase the six TSOC staffs by eight hundred personnel and their budgets by a total of $1 billion, but more will likely be required. The total TSOC staffing for six commands is presently less than that of the single counterterrorism command.
- Theater special operations commands should exercise command and control of all special operations forces and end the practice of separate special operations commands in a single theater or country. This will ensure that all special operations capabilities are employed in an effective, coordinated manner. (This unified military chain of command will continue to fall under the chief of mission's authority except in theaters of war.)
- The Pentagon should work with Congress and the State Department to secure agile, predictable, and adequate funding for sustained special operations and theater campaigns that also incorporates the current reporting requirements to Congress and speedier State Department review for security assistance. This approach would end the practice of different programs competing for funding in a lottery system that leaves some components of a special operations plan unfunded from one year to the next.

DEVISE MORE FLEXIBLE COMBINATIONS OF SPECIAL OPERATIONS AND CONVENTIONAL FORCES

To provide cost-effective and innovative defense options and reduce the danger of overstretch for special operations forces, new ways of combining with conventional forces to conduct small-footprint missions should be devised. The army plans to provide regionally aligned forces to geographic combatant commands on a multiyear timetable, but these formations will need to be highly scalable and tailored to meet the need. To ensure more flexible combinations of special operations forces and conventional forces, the following recommendations should be implemented:

- Senior Defense Department policymakers should mandate the urgent formation of scalable conventional force packages to include "enablers" (such as airlift, intelligence, surveillance, and reconnaissance), "thickeners" (additional infantry), and specialties. These elements should form habitual relationships with special operations units to train and deploy together routinely.
- The U.S. Army Special Operations Command should open its John F. Kennedy Special Warfare Center and School to train as conventional forces advisers, as it has done in the past.

REORIENT INSTITUTIONS AND BUDGET

With support and direction from the secretary of defense, U.S. Special Operations Command should reorient its structure and budget to meet the priorities outlined here. It should increase the proportion and quality of special operations personnel at U.S. Special Operations Command, establish criteria for essential positions to ensure adequate expertise, and prioritize the development of intellectual capital and world-class theater special operations commands. Though the unclassified nature of this study did not permit a close budgetary analysis, various sources suggested that somewhere between one-quarter and one-half of the USSOCOM budget currently devoted to unilateral surgical strike capabilities should be redirected. Top priorities for funding and personnel should include the following:

- U.S. Special Operations Command's new personnel management and development directorate has assumed the most important responsibilities of the command—developing strategy, doctrine, and concepts; leader development and education; and personnel management. Adequate and highly qualified personnel and other resources should be devoted to these foundational endeavors if they are to produce the desired results.

- U.S. Special Operations Command should permanently reassign a significant portion of its 2,606 billets from its Tampa headquarters to fill the gaps at theater special operations commands and redirect funding and resources to make theater special operations commands a world-class capability equipped to fully plan and conduct integrated special operations. In Tampa, the command should reconfigure its remaining staff to prioritize the support it provides to the theater special operations commands in terms of intelligence, planning, and advocacy at the policy, geographic combatant command, and country-team levels to ensure that theater special operations commands are embraced as the primary mechanism for conducting special operations.
- While fulfilling these institutional needs, further study is needed to identify the appropriate operational role for U.S. Special Operations Command and its relationship to geographic combatant commands in today's globalized and networked world. In the interim, the joint staff should ensure that U.S. Special Operations Command has a voice in determining the optimum employment of scarce special operations assets.

To strengthen the ability of the assistant secretary of defense for special operations/low-intensity conflict to carry out his/her legislated functions, the following changes should be made:

- Congress should amend U.S. law (Title 10, Section 138) to strengthen the budget approval authority and other oversight functions of the Office of the Assistant Secretary of Defense for Special Operations/Low-Intensity Conflict, and to make clear that this office is to provide independent advice to the secretary of defense on policy options for employing special operations forces. Additional staff and other measures are needed for this office to keep pace with the policy and oversight responsibilities demanded by a historically large and heavily employed special operations force.
- The assistant secretary of defense for special operations/low-intensity conflict should shed other functions unrelated to his/her statutory duties and focus on policy and resource matters while maintaining sufficient visibility of military operations to provide independent

advice to the secretary of defense. The undersecretary for policy should direct a reorganization of the Office of the Assistant Secretary of Defense for Special Operations/Low-Intensity Conflict to focus its four deputy positions on its statutory functions of policy for special operations/low-intensity conflict and oversight of resources. Other functions should be downgraded to directorates or transferred if they do not pertain to special operations or low-intensity conflict.

Conclusion

Given the centrality of special operations forces in addressing today's national security challenges, it is imperative that they be employed to best effect. The outcome of adopting the changes recommended in this report will be special operations forces that are better prepared to combine effectively within their own community and the wider military, as well as envision how their capabilities can contribute to the U.S. government's national security endeavors around the world.

Current defense strategy envisions a dispersed, small U.S. footprint and emphasizes enabling partners in new ways. This strategy entails a large role for special operations forces, and the changes recommended in this report will provide a force that is capable of fulfilling this role at a higher level and with a more favorable return on investment. That is because special operations forces will, as their core mission, create capable partners and work alongside them in appropriate ways. Those partners will become more proficient more quickly in addressing threats within their own borders and, in time, potential allies in regional or global efforts. All of this will lessen the demand for U.S. special operators over time. This application of special operations forces will lessen the need for direct, unilateral action, which is often controversial and must be applied sparingly. This model also combines special operations capabilities in unified organizations, headed by leaders who are trained and educated in applying the full spectrum of special operations capabilities. Those leaders will be more adept in working within civilian and military structures because they have gained a wider exposure and understanding of national security strategy and policymaking. They will be so equipped because U.S. Special Operations Command performs the vital foundational roles of developing leaders and doctrine and sharing that understanding with government partners. Secrecy has a place in operations, but greater education will benefit those responsible for working with special operations forces.

The broader national security gains to be realized from this further evolution of special operations forces are multiple. The benefits include a greater capacity for achieving enduring solutions rather than temporary Band-Aids or endless campaigns of disruption and decapitation; enhanced security achieved at lower cost with less U.S. presence through increasingly capable partner nations; and a stronger global alliance of partners that avoids a perception of the United States as a unilateralist power that writes its own rules and, in so doing, creates unintended precedents that drive in the opposite direction of declared policy and closely held values.

Enacting these changes to enhance the full range of special operations capabilities will require action by policymakers and Congress. Policymakers should frame the new direction and order a rebalancing of the USSOCOM budget to achieve these goals. Congress has a major role to play on several fronts to ensure that the special operations budget is rebalanced and well-designed plans receive consistent funding. It should also exercise rigorous oversight of special operations and, in particular, monitor clandestine operations that can have widely counterproductive effects if they go awry.

Enacting these changes will be difficult, not only because of bureaucratic inertia but also because there is such a limited view of what special operations forces are. They are the country's premier precision raiders, vital in meeting such urgent contingencies as killing or capturing terrorists, rescuing hostages, and securing weapons of mass destruction. Those capabilities are essential and must be maintained. The recommendations here are additive, to raise the game of special operations forces in enabling and operating with partners in a range of political-military activities, and thereby improving other countries' means to secure themselves. The phrase "You can't kill your way to victory," coined by a special operator, is a useful signpost on the road to a more comprehensive approach to special operations as part of U.S. national security policy.

Appendix:
List of Special Operations Forces Units

U.S. Special Operations Command (USSOCOM) Headquarters
Total assigned strength: 2,606

U.S. Army Special Operations Command
Total assigned strength: 28,500

- U.S. Army John F. Kennedy Special Warfare Center and School: 1,924
- U.S. Army Special Forces Command (Airborne): 11,657
- U.S. Army Special Operations Aviation Command: 3,029
- 75th Ranger Regiment: 3,229
- 4th Military Information Support Group: 729
- 95th Civil Affairs Brigade: 1,266
- 528th Sustainment Brigade (Special Operations): 729
- Special Mission Units: numbers classified

Air Force Special Operations Command
Total assigned strength: 18,000

- Pilots (1st and 27th Special Operations Wings, 352nd and 353rd Special Operations Groups)
- 720th Special Tactics Group:
  – Combat Controllers
  – Pararescue Jumpers
  – Special Operations Weather Teams
  – Tactical Air Control Party

Appendix

Naval Special Warfare Command
Total assigned strength: 9,000

- SEALs
- Special Warfare Combat Crew
- Naval Special Warfare Center

Marine Corps Forces Special Operations Command
Total assigned strength: 2,600

Joint Special Operations Command HQ
Total assigned strength: 1,519

Theater Special Operations Commands HQs
Total assigned strength: 1,425

- Special Operations Command Central
- Special Operations Command Europe
- Special Operations Command Pacific
- Special Operations Command Korea
- Special Operations Command South
- Special Operations Command Africa

Note: Numbers include military and civilians. Numbers approximate as of August 2012.

Endnotes

1. "Sustaining U.S. Global Leadership: Priorities for 21st Century Defense," p. 3. The document was accessed on September 13, 2012, at http://www.defense.gov/news/Defense_Strategic_Guidance.pdf.
2. See *U.S. Special Operations Command FY 2013 Budget Highlights*, p. 6. Accessed October 4, 2012, http://www.socom.mil/News/Documents/USSOCOM_FY_2013_Budget_Highlights.pdf.
3. See the Global Trends reports by the National Intelligence Council, including *Global Trends 2025: A World Transformed*, http://www.dni.gov/index.php/about/organization/national-intelligence-council-global-trends.
4. For example, during the Cold War, the presence of fifty-five advisers in El Salvador in the 1980s was highly controversial but was subsequently credited with playing a significant role in that country's counterinsurgency and the eventual professionalization of its military. Their advisory role was complemented by diplomatic, development, and intelligence assistance.
5. An excellent history of the formation of U.S. Special Operations Command is *Unconventional Warfare: Rebuilding U.S. Special Operations Command* by Susan Marquis (Washington, DC: Brookings Institution Press, 1997). Senators William Cohen (R-ME) and Sam Nunn (D-GA), along with Senate Armed Services Committee senior staff member James R. Locher III, were instrumental in crafting and passing the legislation known as the Cohen-Nunn amendment to the Goldwater-Nichols Defense Reorganization Act.
6. In addition to Africa Command, Pacific Command, and European Command, there is Central Command, which is the geographic combatant command for the Middle East and South Asia, and Southern Command, which oversees activities in Latin America. Pacific Command has two TSOCs, one of which is dedicated to Korea and located in South Korea.
7. Foreign internal defense (FID) is one of the most common but least known missions of special operations forces. It is officially defined in Joint Publication 1-02, the Department of Defense Dictionary of Military and Associated Terms, as "participation by civilian and military agencies of a government in any of the action programs taken by another government or other designated organization, to free and protect its society from subversion, lawlessness, and insurgency." FID is usually undertaken in support of the host nation's plan, which is often referred to as an "internal defense and development (IDAD) plan." The eleven activities undertaken by special operations forces are specified in the current doctrine for special operations, Joint Publication 3-05, II-5-19. A slightly different list of special operations missions is specified in Title 10 USC, Section 167.
8. For example, direct action and special reconnaissance are tactical military activities that may be conducted as part of the operations included in this list (e.g.,

counterterrorism, counterinsurgency, or foreign internal defense). Similarly, civil affairs and information support are usually carried out as supporting activities in the core missions of counterterrorism, counterinsurgency, foreign internal defense, and unconventional warfare.
9. U.S. Special Operations Command Posture Statement, March 6, 2012. Accessed September 13, 2012, http://www.socom.mil/Documents/2012_SOCOM_POSTURE_STATEMENT.pdf. The Army Doctrinal Publication 3-05 on special operations proposes *surgical strike* instead of the direct approach and *special warfare* instead of the indirect approach as terms that are more precise and readily understood.
10. *Surgical strike* connotes small-unit raids or strikes enabled by intelligence and high technology. *Special warfare*, by contrast, entails a variety of activities of a political-military nature that are carried out with and through indigenous actors. These activities may also include "direct action" raids, but they will be carried out with indigenous partners and are more likely to rely primarily on human intelligence. See the Army Doctrinal Publication 3-05. *Surgical* does not mean such strikes are 100 percent accurate. Civilian casualties do still occur, but at much lower rates compared with dumb bombs or the carpet bombing of yore.
11. See the 2012 U.S. Special Operations Command posture statement quoted in the previous section, as well as the annual posture statements of previous years. Though a single raid or a relentless application of raiding may achieve a strategic, decisive, or enduring effect—by destroying the will of the enemy or weakening the enemy to the point of ineffectiveness—the ability of terrorist and insurgent networks to regenerate or metastasize can preclude a definitive outcome. More often, the strategic or decisive impact comes by working through and with others over a lengthy period of time. The reason is simple: raids kill individuals, who can always be replaced, while special warfare, coupled with other efforts, can help change conditions and create forces within countries, thus halting the dynamic that generates new fighters or providing states with means to mitigate or end the conflict.
12. In the case of Special Operations Command Central, it currently has a staff of 303. This is the busiest theater special operations command, given its responsibilities in the tumultuous Middle East and South Asian regions. It has deployed five subordinate commanders to oversee continuing operations in Pakistan, Yemen, Lebanon, Jordan, and the United Arab Emirates. A minimum staff of 523 is required to adequately perform its current functions, according to an official estimate. If the command were to assume control of the special mission task force elements in the region as well, additional staff would be needed. Eighty percent of those interviewed believed theater command structures to be inadequate.
13. The most recent authorities to support special operations forces (SOF) activities are contained in defense authorization bills and referred to by the section in the legislation (Sections 1206, 1207, and 1208), in addition to funding for counternarcotics assistance and joint combined exchange training. By law, the latter must provide a majority benefit to the U.S. forces rather than the partner forces.
14. Title 10 USC Section 138: (4) One of the assistant secretaries is the assistant secretary of defense for special operations/low-intensity conflict. He shall have as his principal duty the overall supervision (including oversight of policy and resources) of special operations activities (as defined in section 167 (j) of this title) and low-intensity conflict activities of the Department of Defense. The assistant secretary is the principal civilian adviser to the secretary of defense on special operations/low-intensity conflict matters and (after the secretary and deputy secretary) is the principal special operations/low-intensity conflict official within the senior management of the Department of Defense.

15. This discussion of special operations draws on Colin Gray's definitions of strategic impact of special operations. See Colin Gray, *Explorations in Strategy* (Santa Barbara, CA: Praeger, 1996). For further discussion of the strategic utility of special operations forces, see Philip Mahla and Christopher Riga, "An Operational Concept for the Transformation of SOF into a Fifth Service" (master's thesis, Naval Postgraduate School, 2003), pp. 15–34, http://edocs.nps.edu/npspubs/scholarly/theses/2003/Jun/03Jun_Mahla.pdf.

About the Author

Linda Robinson is a senior international policy analyst at RAND. In 2011–2012 she was an adjunct senior fellow for U.S. national security and foreign policy at the Council on Foreign Relations, and in 2013 she was a public policy scholar at the Wilson Center. A best-selling author and analyst, Robinson has reported on conflicts, political transitions, and other foreign policy issues around the world, including special operations in Afghanistan, Iraq, Colombia, and elsewhere. Her books include *Tell Me How This Ends: General David Petraeus and the Search for a Way Out of Iraq*; *Masters of Chaos: The Secret History of the Special Forces*; and *Intervention or Neglect: Central America and Panama Beyond the 1980s*. She was previously senior writer for national security and terrorism and Latin America bureau chief at *U.S. News & World Report* and senior editor at *Foreign Affairs* magazine. Robinson coauthored a study on special operations command and control for the U.S. government in 2008–2009. She is currently writing a book on special operations in Afghanistan. Robinson has also been a Nieman fellow at Harvard University, senior consulting fellow at the International Institute for Strategic Studies (IISS), and author-in-residence at the Merrill Center for Strategic Studies at the John Hopkins University's School of Advanced International Studies. She has received the Gerald R. Ford Prize for Distinguished Reporting on National Defense and other awards.

Advisory Committee for
The Future of Special Operations Forces

Stephen D. Biddle, *ex officio*
George Washington University;
Council on Foreign Relations

Max Boot, *ex officio*
Council on Foreign Relations

James F. Dobbins
RAND Corporation

Jeffrey W. Eggers
National Security Council

Andrew Exum
Center for a New American Security

Sherri Goodman
CNA

Lee H. Hamilton
Indiana University

Michele L. Malvesti
Science Applications International
Corporation; Yale University

H. R. McMaster
U.S. Army

David E. Potts
Lockheed Martin Corporation

Theodore Roosevelt IV
Barclays

Nadia Schadlow
Smith Richardson Foundation

Sarah Sewall
Naval War College

Isaiah (Ike) Wilson III
U.S. Military Academy

This report reflects the judgments and recommendations of the author(s). It does not necessarily represent the views of members of the advisory committee, whose involvement in no way should be interpreted as an endorsement of the report by either themselves or the organizations with which they are affiliated.

Council Special Reports
Published by the Council on Foreign Relations

Reforming U.S. Drone Strike Policies
Micah Zenko; CSR No. 65, January 2013
A Center for Preventive Action Report

Countering Criminal Violence in Central America
Michael Shifter; CSR No. 64, April 2012
A Center for Preventive Action Report

Saudi Arabia in the New Middle East
F. Gregory Gause III; CSR No. 63, December 2011
A Center for Preventive Action Report

Partners in Preventive Action: The United States and International Institutions
Paul B. Stares and Micah Zenko; CSR No. 62, September 2011
A Center for Preventive Action Report

Justice Beyond The Hague: Supporting the Prosecution of International Crimes in National Courts
David A. Kaye; CSR No. 61, June 2011

The Drug War in Mexico: Confronting a Shared Threat
David A. Shirk; CSR No. 60, March 2011
A Center for Preventive Action Report

UN Security Council Enlargement and U.S. Interests
Kara C. McDonald and Stewart M. Patrick; CSR No. 59, December 2010
An International Institutions and Global Governance Program Report

Congress and National Security
Kay King; CSR No. 58, November 2010

Toward Deeper Reductions in U.S. and Russian Nuclear Weapons
Micah Zenko; CSR No. 57, November 2010
A Center for Preventive Action Report

Internet Governance in an Age of Cyber Insecurity
Robert K. Knake; CSR No. 56, September 2010
An International Institutions and Global Governance Program Report

From Rome to Kampala: The U.S. Approach to the 2010 International Criminal Court Review Conference
Vijay Padmanabhan; CSR No. 55, April 2010

Strengthening the Nuclear Nonproliferation Regime
Paul Lettow; CSR No. 54, April 2010
An International Institutions and Global Governance Program Report

The Russian Economic Crisis
Jeffrey Mankoff; CSR No. 53, April 2010

Somalia: A New Approach
Bronwyn E. Bruton; CSR No. 52, March 2010
A Center for Preventive Action Report

The Future of NATO
James M. Goldgeier; CSR No. 51, February 2010
An International Institutions and Global Governance Program Report

The United States in the New Asia
Evan A. Feigenbaum and Robert A. Manning; CSR No. 50, November 2009
An International Institutions and Global Governance Program Report

Intervention to Stop Genocide and Mass Atrocities: International Norms and U.S. Policy
Matthew C. Waxman; CSR No. 49, October 2009
An International Institutions and Global Governance Program Report

Enhancing U.S. Preventive Action
Paul B. Stares and Micah Zenko; CSR No. 48, October 2009
A Center for Preventive Action Report

The Canadian Oil Sands: Energy Security vs. Climate Change
Michael A. Levi; CSR No. 47, May 2009
A Maurice R. Greenberg Center for Geoeconomic Studies Report

The National Interest and the Law of the Sea
Scott G. Borgerson; CSR No. 46, May 2009

Lessons of the Financial Crisis
Benn Steil; CSR No. 45, March 2009
A Maurice R. Greenberg Center for Geoeconomic Studies Report

Global Imbalances and the Financial Crisis
Steven Dunaway; CSR No. 44, March 2009
A Maurice R. Greenberg Center for Geoeconomic Studies Report

Eurasian Energy Security
Jeffrey Mankoff; CSR No. 43, February 2009

Preparing for Sudden Change in North Korea
Paul B. Stares and Joel S. Wit; CSR No. 42, January 2009
A Center for Preventive Action Report

Averting Crisis in Ukraine
Steven Pifer; CSR No. 41, January 2009
A Center for Preventive Action Report

Council Special Reports

Congo: Securing Peace, Sustaining Progress
Anthony W. Gambino; CSR No. 40, October 2008
A Center for Preventive Action Report

Deterring State Sponsorship of Nuclear Terrorism
Michael A. Levi; CSR No. 39, September 2008

China, Space Weapons, and U.S. Security
Bruce W. MacDonald; CSR No. 38, September 2008

Sovereign Wealth and Sovereign Power: The Strategic Consequences of American Indebtedness
Brad W. Setser; CSR No. 37, September 2008
A Maurice R. Greenberg Center for Geoeconomic Studies Report

Securing Pakistan's Tribal Belt
Daniel Markey; CSR No. 36, July 2008 (Web-only release) and August 2008
A Center for Preventive Action Report

Avoiding Transfers to Torture
Ashley S. Deeks; CSR No. 35, June 2008

Global FDI Policy: Correcting a Protectionist Drift
David M. Marchick and Matthew J. Slaughter; CSR No. 34, June 2008
A Maurice R. Greenberg Center for Geoeconomic Studies Report

Dealing with Damascus: Seeking a Greater Return on U.S.-Syria Relations
Mona Yacoubian and Scott Lasensky; CSR No. 33, June 2008
A Center for Preventive Action Report

Climate Change and National Security: An Agenda for Action
Joshua W. Busby; CSR No. 32, November 2007
A Maurice R. Greenberg Center for Geoeconomic Studies Report

Planning for Post-Mugabe Zimbabwe
Michelle D. Gavin; CSR No. 31, October 2007
A Center for Preventive Action Report

The Case for Wage Insurance
Robert J. LaLonde; CSR No. 30, September 2007
A Maurice R. Greenberg Center for Geoeconomic Studies Report

Reform of the International Monetary Fund
Peter B. Kenen; CSR No. 29, May 2007
A Maurice R. Greenberg Center for Geoeconomic Studies Report

Nuclear Energy: Balancing Benefits and Risks
Charles D. Ferguson; CSR No. 28, April 2007

Nigeria: Elections and Continuing Challenges
Robert I. Rotberg; CSR No. 27, April 2007
A Center for Preventive Action Report

The Economic Logic of Illegal Immigration
Gordon H. Hanson; CSR No. 26, April 2007
A Maurice R. Greenberg Center for Geoeconomic Studies Report

The United States and the WTO Dispute Settlement System
Robert Z. Lawrence; CSR No. 25, March 2007
A Maurice R. Greenberg Center for Geoeconomic Studies Report

Bolivia on the Brink
Eduardo A. Gamarra; CSR No. 24, February 2007
A Center for Preventive Action Report

After the Surge: The Case for U.S. Military Disengagement from Iraq
Steven N. Simon; CSR No. 23, February 2007

Darfur and Beyond: What Is Needed to Prevent Mass Atrocities
Lee Feinstein; CSR No. 22, January 2007

Avoiding Conflict in the Horn of Africa: U.S. Policy Toward Ethiopia and Eritrea
Terrence Lyons; CSR No. 21, December 2006
A Center for Preventive Action Report

Living with Hugo: U.S. Policy Toward Hugo Chávez's Venezuela
Richard Lapper; CSR No. 20, November 2006
A Center for Preventive Action Report

Reforming U.S. Patent Policy: Getting the Incentives Right
Keith E. Maskus; CSR No. 19, November 2006
A Maurice R. Greenberg Center for Geoeconomic Studies Report

Foreign Investment and National Security: Getting the Balance Right
Alan P. Larson and David M. Marchick; CSR No. 18, July 2006
A Maurice R. Greenberg Center for Geoeconomic Studies Report

Challenges for a Postelection Mexico: Issues for U.S. Policy
Pamela K. Starr; CSR No. 17, June 2006 (Web-only release) and November 2006

U.S.-India Nuclear Cooperation: A Strategy for Moving Forward
Michael A. Levi and Charles D. Ferguson; CSR No. 16, June 2006

Generating Momentum for a New Era in U.S.-Turkey Relations
Steven A. Cook and Elizabeth Sherwood-Randall; CSR No. 15, June 2006

Peace in Papua: Widening a Window of Opportunity
Blair A. King; CSR No. 14, March 2006
A Center for Preventive Action Report

Neglected Defense: Mobilizing the Private Sector to Support Homeland Security
Stephen E. Flynn and Daniel B. Prieto; CSR No. 13, March 2006

Afghanistan's Uncertain Transition From Turmoil to Normalcy
Barnett R. Rubin; CSR No. 12, March 2006
A Center for Preventive Action Report

Preventing Catastrophic Nuclear Terrorism
Charles D. Ferguson; CSR No. 11, March 2006

Getting Serious About the Twin Deficits
Menzie D. Chinn; CSR No. 10, September 2005
A Maurice R. Greenberg Center for Geoeconomic Studies Report

Both Sides of the Aisle: A Call for Bipartisan Foreign Policy
Nancy E. Roman; CSR No. 9, September 2005

Forgotten Intervention? What the United States Needs to Do in the Western Balkans
Amelia Branczik and William L. Nash; CSR No. 8, June 2005
A Center for Preventive Action Report

A New Beginning: Strategies for a More Fruitful Dialogue with the Muslim World
Craig Charney and Nicole Yakatan; CSR No. 7, May 2005

Power-Sharing in Iraq
David L. Phillips; CSR No. 6, April 2005
A Center for Preventive Action Report

Giving Meaning to "Never Again": Seeking an Effective Response to the Crisis in Darfur and Beyond
Cheryl O. Igiri and Princeton N. Lyman; CSR No. 5, September 2004

Freedom, Prosperity, and Security: The G8 Partnership with Africa: Sea Island 2004 and Beyond
J. Brian Atwood, Robert S. Browne, and Princeton N. Lyman; CSR No. 4, May 2004

Addressing the HIV/AIDS Pandemic: A U.S. Global AIDS Strategy for the Long Term
Daniel M. Fox and Princeton N. Lyman; CSR No. 3, May 2004
Cosponsored with the Milbank Memorial Fund

Challenges for a Post-Election Philippines
Catharin E. Dalpino; CSR No. 2, May 2004
A Center for Preventive Action Report

Stability, Security, and Sovereignty in the Republic of Georgia
David L. Phillips; CSR No. 1, January 2004
A Center for Preventive Action Report

Note: Council Special Reports are available for download from CFR's website, www.cfr.org. For more information, email publications@cfr.org.

www.ingramcontent.com/pod-product-compliance
Lightning Source LLC
Chambersburg PA
CBHW070040070426
42449CB00012BA/3121